■SCHOLASTIC
News
Nonfiction Readers

Math in the Neighborhood

by Ellen Weiss

Children's Press®
A Division of Scholastic Inc.
New York Toronto London Auckland Sydney
Mexico City New Delhi Hong Kong
Danbury, Connecticut

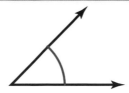

These content vocabulary word builders are for grades 1–2.

Math Consultant: Linda K. Voges, EdD, Cohort Coordinator/Lecturer,
College of Education, The University of Texas at Austin

Reading Consultant: Cecilia Minden-Cupp, PhD, Early Literacy Consultant and Author,
Chapel Hill, North Carolina

Photographs © 2008: age fotostock/SW Productions: cover; James Levin Studios: 9;
PhotoEdit: 4 bottom left, 8 (Bill Aron), 13 (Richard Hutchings), 5 bottom right, 17, 19
(Colin Young-Wolff); The Image Works/Bob Daemmrich: back cover, 1, 7.

Illustrations by Kathy Petelinsek

Book Design: Simonsays Design!
Book Production: The Design Lab

Library of Congress Cataloging-in-Publication Data
Weiss, Ellen, 1949–
Math in the Neighborhood / by Ellen Weiss.
    p. cm.—(Scholastic news nonfiction readers)
Includes bibliographical references and index.
ISBN-13: 978-0-531-18532-2 (lib. bdg.) 978-0-531-18785-2 (pbk.)
ISBN-10: 0-531-18532-X (lib. bdg.) 0-531-18785-3 (pbk.)
1. Mathematics—Juvenile literature. 2. Neighborhood—Juvenile litera-
    ture. I. Title. II. Series.
QA40.5.W446 2008
510—dc22   2007005694

CONTENTS

WORD HUNT

Look for these words as you read. They will be in **bold**.

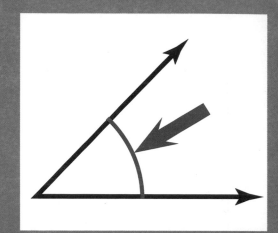

angle
(**an**-gul)

measurements
(**meh**-zhur-ments)

hour	minutes
8:	10, 20, 30, 40,
9:	15, 30, 45
10:	15, 30, 45
11:	15, 30, 45
12:	15, 30, 45
1:	15, 30, 45

minutes
(**mi**-nuts)

corner
(**kor**-nur)

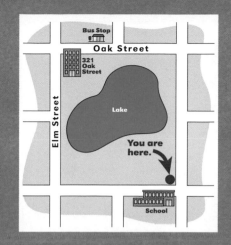

map
(map)

ramp
(ramp)

timetable
(**time**-tay-buhl)

Neighborhood Numbers

Math is all around us!

Let's walk home from school today.

Let's see where we can find math at work.

This builder is working on a new house. He uses math every step of the way.

He uses **measurements** to figure out how much wood to buy.

He also uses math to count nails and boards.

measurements

The builder is holding papers called blueprints. The blueprints show all the measurements he needs!

The builder is making a **ramp**.

The top of the ramp and the ground will form an **angle**.

An angle is made by two lines that start at the same point.

The builder has a picture of the angle he needs. This angle will make a ramp that reaches the door.

Match the ramp's angle to one of these.

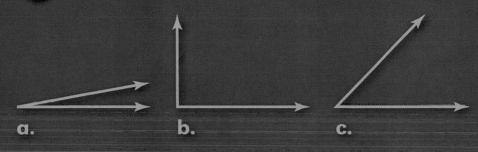

a. **b.** **c.**

PLAN FOR RAMP

angle

ramp

Turn to page 23 for the answer.

We walk home from school with our friends.

We see angles on every corner.

We see shapes, too.

It's fun to walk through the neighborhood together.

Soon we will be at our friend's building.

An octagon has eight sides and angles.
Can you see the octagon in this picture?

Our friend lives at 321 Oak Street.

That is near the **corner** of Oak Street and Elm Street.

Can you help us find the way?

Use this **map**.

Trace our path with your finger. How many blocks do we have to walk?

Turn to page 23 for the answer.

Neighborhood Map

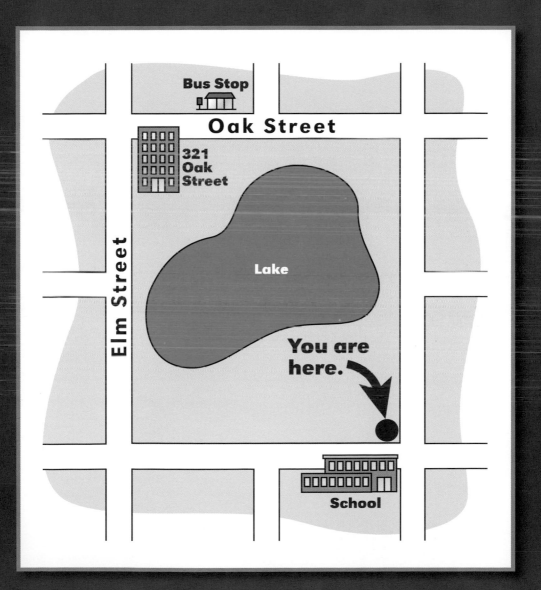

This man walks our neighbor's dogs.

He just took three dogs home.

Count the dogs he has left.

How many dogs did he walk today?

Turn to page 23 for the answer.

**Three dogs are here.
Three dogs are home.
3 + 3 = ?**

Now we are almost home.

We can see the bus stop on our street.

At the bus stop, there's a **timetable**.

The timetable is a chart that shows when the buses will arrive.

It says the bus comes at 4:15, 4:30, and 4:45 p.m.

big blue bus

timetable

Our watch says it's 4:21.

Mom comes home from work on the 4:30 bus.

Let's wait for her at the bus stop!

How many **minutes** is it until her bus comes?

Soon we will be home for supper!

Turn to page 23 for the answer.

Timetable for Bus Route 1

	hour	minutes
A.M.	8:	10, 20, 30, 40, 50
	9:	15, 30, 45
	10:	15, 30, 45
	11:	15, 30, 45
P.M.	12:	15, 30, 45
	1:	15, 30, 45
	2:	15, 30, 45
	3:	15, 30, 45
	4:	15, (30,) 45
	5:	10, 20, 30, 40, 50
	6:	15, 30, 45

30 - 21 = ?

INDEX

FIND OUT MORE

Book:

Keenan, Sheila, and Kayne Jacobs (illustrator). *What Time Is It? A Book of Math Riddles.* New York: Scholastic, 1999.

Website:

FunBrain.com—Math Arcade
www.funbrain.com/brain/MathBrain/MathBrain.html

MEET THE AUTHOR

Ellen Weiss has received many awards for her books for kids. She lived in England for a short time, where people say "maths" instead of "math."